EMMANUEL JOSEPH

Divine Dreams, Shaping Godly, Moral Entrepreneurs of Tomorrow

Copyright © 2025 by Emmanuel Joseph

All rights reserved. No part of this publication may be reproduced, stored or transmitted in any form or by any means, electronic, mechanical, photocopying, recording, scanning, or otherwise without written permission from the publisher. It is illegal to copy this book, post it to a website, or distribute it by any other means without permission.

First edition

This book was professionally typeset on Reedsy. Find out more at reedsy.com

Contents

1	Chapter 1	1
2	Chapter 1: The Spark of Vision	3
3	Chapter 2: Building a Foundation	4
4	Chapter 3: Embracing Challenges	5
5	Chapter 4: Cultivating Innovation	6
6	Chapter 5: Leading with Compassion	7
7	Chapter 6: Navigating Ethical Dilemmas	8
8	Chapter 7: Empowering Others	9
9	Chapter 8: Balancing Work and Faith	10
10	Chapter 9: Celebrating Success	11
11	Chapter 10: Overcoming Adversity	12
12	Chapter 11: Fostering Community	13
13	Chapter 12: Sustaining Growth	14
14	Chapter 13: Passing the Torch	15
15	Chapter 14: Reflecting on the Journey	16
16	Chapter 15: Embracing the Future	17
17	Chapter 16: Expanding Horizons	18
18	Chapter 17: Harnessing Technology	19
19	Chapter 18: Promoting Sustainability	20
20	Chapter 19: Embracing Diversity	21
21	Chapter 20: Nurturing Relationships	22
22	Chapter 21: Giving Back	23
23	Chapter 22: Honoring Traditions	24
24	Chapter 23: Inspiring Innovation	25
25	Chapter 24: Building Resilience	26
26	Chapter 25: Embracing Legacy	27

1

Chapter 1

Introduction

In a world where business and morality often seem at odds, **Divine Dreams: Shaping Godly, Moral Entrepreneurs of Tomorrow** seeks to bridge the gap and inspire a new generation of ethical entrepreneurs. This book tells the story of Celeste, a visionary young woman whose unwavering faith and strong moral compass guide her entrepreneurial journey. Set in the charming town of Harmonyville, Celeste's tale is one of resilience, innovation, and compassion, offering valuable lessons for anyone looking to integrate their spiritual beliefs with their professional endeavors.

Celeste's journey begins with a spark of inspiration, ignited by her mentor, Father Gabriel. His teachings on stewardship and moral entrepreneurship lay the foundation for Celeste's business ventures. Father Gabriel's wisdom, drawn from biblical entrepreneurs like Joseph and Lydia, provides Celeste with a blueprint for success that goes beyond mere profit. Through her faith-driven approach, Celeste learns that true success is measured by the positive impact one can make on the world.

As Celeste embarks on her entrepreneurial journey, she faces numerous challenges that test her faith and determination. From navigating economic downturns to making difficult ethical decisions, Celeste's story is a testament to the power of resilience and integrity. Her bakery, Heavenly Delights, becomes a beacon of hope in Harmonyville, demonstrating that businesses can thrive while upholding ethical practices and contributing to the greater good.

Throughout the book, readers will find themselves immersed in a series of heartwarming and inspiring stories that highlight the importance of maintaining integrity in business. Celeste's encounters with mentors, customers, and fellow entrepreneurs offer valuable insights into the principles and practices that can shape ethical and successful entrepreneurs. Each chapter is filled with practical advice, drawn from Celeste's experiences and the wisdom of her mentors, providing readers with a roadmap for their own entrepreneurial journeys.

In addition to practical guidance, **Divine Dreams** delves into the spiritual dimension of entrepreneurship. Celeste's faith is a constant source of strength and guidance, helping her navigate the complexities of the business world. The book explores how godly principles can shape ethical decision-making and provide a sense of purpose and direction. Celeste's story is a powerful reminder that success is not just about achieving financial goals but about fulfilling a higher purpose and making a positive impact on the world.

As readers follow Celeste's journey, they will be inspired to dream big and pursue their own entrepreneurial endeavors with faith, integrity, and compassion. The lessons learned from Celeste's experiences are timeless and applicable to entrepreneurs of all ages and backgrounds. **Divine Dreams: Shaping Godly, Moral Entrepreneurs of Tomorrow** is more than just a book; it is a call to action for those who seek to create businesses that reflect their godly values and contribute to the greater good.

Through Celeste's story, this book aims to inspire a new generation of ethical entrepreneurs who are committed to making a difference. By embracing the divine dreams within us and striving to shape a brighter, more ethical future, we can create a world where business and morality go hand in hand. Join Celeste on her journey and discover the transformative power of faith, integrity, and compassion in the world of entrepreneurship.

2

Chapter 1: The Spark of Vision

In the quiet town of Harmonyville, young Celeste often found herself lost in dreams of a world filled with possibility. Each dream was a divine whisper, inspiring her to envision a life where business and faith were intertwined. Her journey began with a mentor, Father Gabriel, whose teachings on stewardship and entrepreneurship ignited a spark within her. Father Gabriel believed that true success was rooted in moral values and a godly vision, a philosophy he imparted to his eager protégée. Celeste's first venture, a humble bakery, became a testament to her unwavering faith and determination.

Father Gabriel shared stories of biblical entrepreneurs, like Joseph who became a trusted advisor in Egypt, and Lydia, a successful merchant of purple cloth. These tales resonated with Celeste, who saw them as divine blueprints for her own path. Her bakery, Heavenly Delights, quickly became a beacon of hope and inspiration in Harmonyville. Customers marveled not only at the delicious treats but also at the warmth and kindness that filled the air. Celeste's journey was just beginning, and her faith would guide her every step of the way.

3

Chapter 2: Building a Foundation

As Heavenly Delights flourished, Celeste realized that a solid foundation was essential for sustained success. She sought advice from seasoned entrepreneurs, attended workshops, and immersed herself in the study of business ethics. One of her mentors, Mr. Thompson, emphasized the importance of integrity in every transaction. He shared a story about his own business venture, where a decision to uphold honesty over profit earned him the respect and loyalty of his clients. This lesson resonated deeply with Celeste, reinforcing her commitment to moral principles.

Celeste's bakery expanded, and she employed a team of passionate individuals who shared her vision. She ensured that every team member understood the core values of the business: honesty, compassion, and excellence. Together, they created a workplace culture that celebrated faith and integrity. As the bakery's reputation grew, Celeste's commitment to ethical practices became a model for aspiring entrepreneurs in Harmonyville. She often reminded her team that their actions, no matter how small, could have a profound impact on the lives of others.

4

Chapter 3: Embracing Challenges

No journey is without its challenges, and Celeste faced her fair share of obstacles. A sudden economic downturn threatened to derail her dreams, but she turned to prayer and sought guidance from her church community. Father Gabriel's words echoed in her mind: "Trust in God's plan, even when the path seems unclear." With renewed faith, Celeste devised creative solutions to keep her business afloat. She introduced new products, collaborated with local farmers, and launched a series of community events to attract customers.

One memorable event was the "Harvest Festival," where local artisans showcased their crafts and musicians filled the air with joyful melodies. The festival not only boosted the bakery's sales but also strengthened the sense of community in Harmonyville. Celeste's resilience and unwavering faith inspired others to persevere through their own struggles. Her story spread beyond the town, and she received invitations to speak at conferences and share her experiences with aspiring entrepreneurs. Celeste's journey was a testament to the power of faith and determination in overcoming adversity.

5

Chapter 4: Cultivating Innovation

Innovation became a cornerstone of Celeste's entrepreneurial journey. She believed that creativity, guided by godly principles, could lead to transformative solutions. Celeste invested in research and development, exploring new recipes and sustainable practices. She collaborated with experts in nutrition to create healthy and delicious treats, catering to diverse dietary needs. One of her most successful innovations was the "Heavenly Health" line, which featured gluten-free, vegan, and low-sugar options.

Celeste also embraced technology, implementing digital marketing strategies to reach a wider audience. She launched an e-commerce platform, allowing customers to order their favorite treats online. Her innovative approach not only increased sales but also provided valuable insights into customer preferences. Celeste's bakery became a hub of creativity, where team members were encouraged to share their ideas and experiment with new concepts. The spirit of innovation, grounded in faith and morality, drove the bakery's continued success and growth.

Chapter 5: Leading with Compassion

Leadership, for Celeste, was synonymous with compassion. She believed that a true leader served others with humility and grace. Celeste's leadership style was deeply influenced by her faith, and she often drew inspiration from the teachings of Jesus. She treated her team with respect and kindness, fostering an environment where everyone felt valued and supported. Celeste implemented flexible work schedules, provided opportunities for professional development, and prioritized the well-being of her employees.

One heartwarming story involved an employee, Maria, who faced a family crisis. Celeste not only offered her time off but also organized a fundraiser to support Maria's family. The outpouring of generosity from the community was overwhelming, and Maria's gratitude knew no bounds. Celeste's compassionate leadership created a ripple effect, inspiring others to act with kindness and empathy. Her bakery became a place where individuals found not just employment but also a sense of belonging and purpose.

7

Chapter 6: Navigating Ethical Dilemmas

Ethical dilemmas are an inevitable part of any entrepreneurial journey, and Celeste was no exception. One significant challenge arose when a supplier offered her a lucrative deal that involved questionable practices. Torn between profit and principle, Celeste sought counsel from Father Gabriel and her trusted mentors. She prayed for wisdom and clarity, ultimately deciding to reject the deal. This decision, though difficult, reaffirmed her commitment to ethical conduct and earned her the respect of her community.

Celeste's integrity attracted like-minded partners and investors who shared her values. She formed alliances with ethical suppliers and businesses, creating a network of trust and mutual support. One such partnership was with Green Farms, a local organic farm that provided fresh ingredients for the bakery. The collaboration not only ensured high-quality products but also supported sustainable and environmentally-friendly practices. Celeste's unwavering commitment to ethics became a guiding light for other entrepreneurs, inspiring them to prioritize integrity over profit.

8

Chapter 7: Empowering Others

Empowerment was at the heart of Celeste's mission. She believed in the potential of every individual to make a positive impact on the world. Celeste organized workshops and mentorship programs for aspiring entrepreneurs, sharing her knowledge and experiences. She invited guest speakers, including successful business leaders and faith-based influencers, to inspire and educate the participants. One of the most memorable workshops was "Entrepreneurial Faith," which explored the intersection of spirituality and business.

Celeste also launched a scholarship program for underprivileged youth, providing them with opportunities to pursue their entrepreneurial dreams. One scholarship recipient, Samuel, went on to start a successful tech company that developed innovative solutions for small businesses. His journey was a testament to the transformative power of empowerment and mentorship. Celeste's dedication to nurturing the next generation of entrepreneurs created a ripple effect, spreading hope and inspiration far beyond Harmonyville.

9

Chapter 8: Balancing Work and Faith

Balancing work and faith was a constant endeavor for Celeste. She believed that success in business should not come at the expense of one's spiritual well-being. Celeste dedicated time each day for prayer, reflection, and Bible study. She also encouraged her team to take breaks and participate in faith-based activities. One of her favorite practices was the "Morning Devotion," where the team gathered to start the day with a prayer and a reflection on a scripture passage.

Celeste's faith was a source of strength and guidance, helping her navigate the complexities of entrepreneurship. She often turned to the Proverbs for wisdom, finding solace in verses like Proverbs 3:5-6, "Trust in the Lord with all your heart and lean not on your own understanding; in all your ways submit to him, and he will make your paths straight." Celeste's commitment to balancing work and faith created a harmonious and fulfilling life, serving as a model for others seeking to integrate their spiritual beliefs with their professional pursuits.

Chapter 9: Celebrating Success

Celebrating success was an integral part of Celeste's journey. She believed that achievements, both big and small, deserved recognition and gratitude. Celeste organized annual "Heavenly Awards" to honor the hard work and dedication of her team. The awards ceremony was a joyous occasion, filled with laughter, music, and heartfelt speeches. One year, the "Employee of the Year" award went to John, a loyal and passionate baker who had been with the company since its inception.

Celeste also celebrated the milestones of her business, such as the opening of new branches and the launch of innovative products. Each celebration was an opportunity to reflect on the journey, express gratitude to God, and acknowledge the contributions of the community. Celeste's bakery became known for its vibrant and inclusive culture, where success was shared and celebrated. Her approach to recognizing and appreciating achievements fostered a sense of pride and motivation among her team.

11

Chapter 10: Overcoming Adversity

Adversity tested Celeste's faith and resilience, but she remained steadfast in her belief that challenges were opportunities for growth. One significant trial came in the form of a devastating fire that destroyed the bakery. The loss was overwhelming, but Celeste's community rallied around her, offering support and assistance. Father Gabriel's words of comfort and encouragement gave her the strength to rebuild. "God is with you in every storm," he reminded her.

With the help of her team and the generosity of her community, Celeste began the process of rebuilding the bakery. They worked tirelessly, transforming the ashes into a new and improved Heavenly Delights. The grand reopening was a celebration of resilience and hope, with tears of joy and heartfelt gratitude. Celeste's story of overcoming adversity became an inspiration to many, demonstrating the power of faith and community in the face of hardship.

Chapter 11: Fostering Community

Celeste believed that a business could be a force for good in the community. She actively engaged with local organizations, schools, and churches, fostering partnerships that benefited everyone. One notable initiative was the "Bread for All" program, where the bakery donated surplus bread to homeless shelters and food banks. This program not only addressed food insecurity but also strengthened the bonds within the community. Celeste's bakery became a place where people from all walks of life felt welcome and valued.

Celeste also organized community events, such as bake sales for charity, holiday celebrations, and educational workshops. One memorable event was the "Faith and Business Summit," which brought together entrepreneurs, faith leaders, and community members to discuss the role of faith in business. The summit featured inspiring speakers, interactive sessions, and networking opportunities, creating a platform for meaningful dialogue and collaboration. Celeste's efforts to foster community created a sense of belonging and unity, making Harmonyville a better place for everyone.

13

Chapter 12: Sustaining Growth

Sustaining growth required careful planning and strategic thinking. Celeste was committed to scaling her business while staying true to her values. She sought advice from experienced business leaders and prayed for guidance in making important decisions. One of her mentors, Mrs. Edwards, shared valuable insights on scaling ethically. She emphasized the importance of maintaining quality and integrity, even as the business expanded. This advice resonated with Celeste, who was determined to uphold her moral principles.

Celeste implemented sustainable practices, such as using eco-friendly packaging and sourcing ingredients from local farmers. She also invested in employee training and development, ensuring that her team was equipped to handle the challenges of growth. The bakery expanded to new locations, each one reflecting the same commitment to quality and community. Celeste's approach to sustainable growth became a model for other businesses, demonstrating that it was possible to achieve success without compromising on values.

Chapter 13: Passing the Torch

As Celeste's journey progressed, she began to think about the future and the legacy she wanted to leave behind. She believed in the importance of mentorship and was committed to passing on her knowledge and experiences to the next generation. Celeste identified promising young entrepreneurs and took them under her wing, providing guidance, support, and opportunities for growth. One of her protégés, Grace, showed great potential and shared Celeste's passion for faith-based entrepreneurship.

Celeste worked closely with Grace, teaching her the intricacies of the business and the importance of ethical conduct. Together, they launched a new venture, "Divine Delights," a bakery that combined traditional recipes with innovative twists. Grace's energy and creativity breathed new life into the business, and Celeste felt a sense of fulfillment in knowing that her legacy would continue. The mentorship relationship between Celeste and Grace exemplified the power of passing the torch and empowering the next generation.

15

Chapter 14: Reflecting on the Journey

Celeste often took time to reflect on her journey and the lessons she had learned along the way. She kept a journal, recording her thoughts, prayers, and experiences. Each entry was a testament to her faith, resilience, and determination. Celeste believed that reflection was essential for personal and spiritual growth. It allowed her to appreciate the progress she had made and to seek guidance for the future.

One evening, as Celeste sat in her favorite spot by the window, she reflected on the impact her bakery had made on the community. She thought about the countless lives she had touched, the friendships she had forged, and the dreams she had inspired. Celeste's heart swelled with gratitude as she realized that her journey was not just about business but about fulfilling a divine purpose. Her reflections deepened her faith and strengthened her resolve to continue living out her godly vision.

16

Chapter 15: Embracing the Future

The future was bright and filled with endless possibilities for Celeste and her bakery. She continued to innovate, explore new markets, and expand her impact. Celeste's vision of a world where business and faith coexisted harmoniously was becoming a reality. She remained committed to her values, knowing that her faith would guide her through any challenges that lay ahead. Celeste's journey was far from over, and she looked forward to the new adventures and opportunities that awaited her.

One of her future projects was the "Faithful Entrepreneurs Network," a platform that connected faith-based business leaders from around the world. The network provided resources, mentorship, and support for entrepreneurs who wanted to integrate their faith into their business practices. Celeste's vision was to create a global community of godly, moral entrepreneurs who would inspire positive change in the world. As she embraced the future, Celeste knew that her divine dreams would continue to shape the entrepreneurs of tomorrow.

17

Chapter 16: Expanding Horizons

Celeste knew that growth required looking beyond her familiar surroundings. She embarked on a journey to explore new markets and learn from different cultures. Her travels took her to bustling cities and remote villages, where she met entrepreneurs with diverse experiences. One memorable encounter was with Amina, a young woman from a small village in Nigeria, who had started a successful business making traditional crafts. Amina's story of resilience and innovation inspired Celeste to think creatively about expanding her own business.

Celeste returned to Harmonyville with a wealth of knowledge and new ideas. She introduced products that incorporated international flavors and techniques, appealing to a broader audience. Her bakery's new line, "Global Delights," featured treats inspired by her travels, such as matcha green tea cookies from Japan and spiced mango muffins from India. Celeste's willingness to expand her horizons and embrace diversity enriched her business and connected her with a global community of like-minded individuals.

18

Chapter 17: Harnessing Technology

In an increasingly digital world, Celeste recognized the importance of leveraging technology to enhance her business. She invested in cutting-edge tools and platforms to streamline operations and improve customer experience. One significant innovation was the implementation of a customer relationship management (CRM) system, which allowed her to better understand her customers' preferences and personalize their experiences. Celeste also embraced social media, using it to engage with her audience and share the bakery's story.

Celeste's tech-savvy approach extended to her team as well. She provided training on digital tools and encouraged her employees to embrace new technologies. One notable success was the development of a mobile app for the bakery, which offered customers the convenience of ordering online and receiving updates on new products and promotions. The app became a hit, attracting tech-savvy customers and boosting sales. Celeste's ability to harness technology while staying true to her values set her apart as an innovative and forward-thinking entrepreneur.

19

Chapter 18: Promoting Sustainability

Sustainability became a core focus for Celeste, who believed that businesses had a responsibility to protect the environment. She implemented eco-friendly practices in every aspect of her bakery, from sourcing ingredients to packaging products. Celeste partnered with local farmers who used sustainable farming methods, ensuring that her ingredients were fresh and environmentally friendly. She also introduced biodegradable packaging and reduced waste through recycling and composting initiatives.

Celeste's commitment to sustainability extended to her community as well. She organized events to raise awareness about environmental issues and encourage sustainable practices. One such event was the "Green Fair," where local businesses and organizations showcased their eco-friendly products and services. The fair included workshops on topics such as organic gardening, renewable energy, and waste reduction. Celeste's dedication to sustainability not only benefited the environment but also inspired others to take action and make a positive impact.

20

Chapter 19: Embracing Diversity

Diversity was a value that Celeste cherished deeply. She believed that a diverse team brought a wealth of perspectives and ideas, enriching the business and fostering innovation. Celeste actively sought to create an inclusive and welcoming environment, where individuals from all backgrounds felt valued and respected. She implemented diversity training programs and promoted policies that encouraged equal opportunities for everyone.

Celeste's commitment to diversity was reflected in her hiring practices and workplace culture. She welcomed team members from different cultures, ethnicities, and backgrounds, creating a melting pot of talents and experiences. This diversity was also evident in the bakery's products, which celebrated a wide range of flavors and culinary traditions. Celeste's inclusive approach not only strengthened her business but also created a sense of unity and belonging among her team and customers.

Chapter 20: Nurturing Relationships

Relationships were at the heart of Celeste's entrepreneurial journey. She believed that strong, authentic connections with customers, employees, and partners were essential for long-term success. Celeste prioritized building and nurturing these relationships, taking the time to understand and appreciate the people who contributed to her business. She often organized team-building activities, customer appreciation events, and partnership gatherings to strengthen these bonds.

One heartwarming story involved a long-time customer, Mrs. Johnson, who visited the bakery every week for her favorite lemon tarts. When Mrs. Johnson celebrated her 80th birthday, Celeste organized a surprise party at the bakery, inviting her family and friends. The celebration was filled with joy and gratitude, as Mrs. Johnson expressed her appreciation for the bakery's role in her life. Celeste's ability to nurture relationships created a loyal and supportive community, contributing to the bakery's enduring success.

22

Chapter 21: Giving Back

Celeste believed in the importance of giving back to the community that had supported her business. She initiated various philanthropic efforts, from donating to local charities to volunteering her time and resources. One significant initiative was the "Heavenly Scholars" program, which provided scholarships and mentorship to underprivileged youth. The program aimed to empower young individuals to pursue their dreams and achieve their full potential.

Celeste also partnered with organizations that focused on social causes, such as homelessness, education, and healthcare. She organized fundraisers, donation drives, and awareness campaigns to support these causes. One memorable event was the "Run for Hope," a charity run that raised funds for a local orphanage. The event brought together the entire community, with participants of all ages running to make a difference. Celeste's commitment to giving back created a legacy of generosity and compassion, inspiring others to contribute to the greater good.

23

Chapter 22: Honoring Traditions

While innovation and growth were important, Celeste also valued the significance of traditions. She believed that honoring traditions created a sense of continuity and connection to the past. Celeste incorporated family recipes and time-honored techniques into her bakery's offerings, preserving the flavors and memories of generations. One cherished recipe was her grandmother's apple pie, a customer favorite that evoked nostalgia and warmth.

Celeste also celebrated cultural and religious traditions, organizing special events and promotions for holidays such as Christmas, Easter, and Thanksgiving. The bakery became a gathering place for families and friends, who came together to share the joy and meaning of these celebrations. Celeste's ability to honor traditions while embracing the future created a unique and cherished experience for her customers, blending the best of both worlds.

24

Chapter 23: Inspiring Innovation

Celeste's journey was marked by a continuous pursuit of innovation. She believed that creativity and forward-thinking were essential for staying ahead in the competitive business world. Celeste encouraged her team to think outside the box and experiment with new ideas. She organized brainstorming sessions and innovation labs, where team members could collaborate and explore possibilities. One successful innovation was the "Seasonal Surprises" line, which featured limited-edition products inspired by the changing seasons.

Celeste also stayed informed about industry trends and technological advancements, attending conferences and networking with experts. Her dedication to innovation led to the development of unique products and services that set her bakery apart from the competition. Celeste's ability to inspire innovation and foster a culture of creativity ensured that her business remained dynamic and relevant in an ever-evolving market.

Chapter 24: Building Resilience

Resilience was a quality that Celeste embodied throughout her entrepreneurial journey. She believed that the ability to adapt and persevere in the face of challenges was crucial for long-term success. Celeste faced numerous setbacks, from economic downturns to natural disasters, but she remained steadfast in her faith and determination. She viewed each challenge as an opportunity to learn and grow, drawing strength from her faith and the support of her community.

Celeste implemented strategies to build resilience within her business, such as diversifying revenue streams, maintaining strong cash reserves, and developing contingency plans. She also prioritized the well-being of her team, providing support and resources to help them navigate difficult times. Celeste's resilience inspired others to stay strong in the face of adversity and created a culture of perseverance and optimism within her business.

26

Chapter 25: Embracing Legacy

As Celeste's journey neared a new chapter, she reflected on the legacy she wanted to leave behind. She believed that her business was more than just a bakery; it was a testament to faith, integrity, and compassion. Celeste documented her experiences and insights in a book, sharing her story with a wider audience. The book, titled "Divine Dreams: Shaping Godly, Moral Entrepreneurs of Tomorrow," became a source of inspiration and guidance for aspiring entrepreneurs.

Celeste also established a foundation to continue her philanthropic efforts and support the causes she cared about. The "Celeste Foundation" provided grants and resources to initiatives that aligned with her values, such as education, sustainability, and community development. Celeste's legacy was one of hope, empowerment, and positive impact, creating a ripple effect that would continue to inspire and uplift others for generations to come.

Description
Divine Dreams: Shaping Godly, Moral Entrepreneurs of Tomorrow is an inspiring and heartfelt journey into the world of faith-based entrepreneurship. Through the captivating story of Celeste, a visionary young woman with a passion for integrating her faith into her business ventures, this book offers valuable insights and practical advice for aspiring entrepreneurs.

Set in the quaint town of Harmonyville, Celeste's journey begins with the guidance of her mentor, Father Gabriel, whose teachings on stewardship and moral entrepreneurship lay the foundation for her success. As Celeste navigates the challenges and triumphs of building her bakery, Heavenly Delights, she learns that true success is measured not just by profit but by the positive impact one can make on the world.

Throughout the book, readers will find themselves immersed in a series of heartwarming and inspiring stories that highlight the importance of integrity, resilience, and compassion in business. Celeste's encounters with mentors, customers, and fellow entrepreneurs offer valuable lessons on maintaining ethical practices and staying true to one's principles.

In addition to practical guidance, **Divine Dreams** delves into the spiritual dimension of entrepreneurship, exploring how faith can provide strength and direction in times of uncertainty. Celeste's unwavering faith and dedication to her values serve as a powerful reminder that success is not just about achieving financial goals but about fulfilling a higher purpose and making a positive impact on the world.

As readers follow Celeste's journey, they will be inspired to dream big and pursue their own entrepreneurial endeavors with faith, integrity, and compassion. **Divine Dreams: Shaping Godly, Moral Entrepreneurs of Tomorrow** is more than just a book; it is a call to action for those who seek to create businesses that reflect their godly values and contribute to the greater good.

Join Celeste on her journey and discover the transformative power of faith, integrity, and compassion in the world of entrepreneurship. Let this book inspire you to embrace your own divine dreams and shape a brighter, more ethical future for the entrepreneurs of tomorrow.

www.ingramcontent.com/pod-product-compliance
Lightning Source LLC
LaVergne TN
LVHW010444070526
838199LV00066B/6178